unmask

SABRA BRYANT SKIDMORE

FULL CIRCLE · FULL CIRCLE·

FULL CIRCLE: unmask

Copyright © 2024 (Sabra Bryant Skidmore) Full Circle Ministries
www.sabraskidmore.com

ISBN: 9798328069502
Printed in the United States of America

All rights reserved. No part of this publication may be reproduced or transmitted in any form or by any means, electronic or mechanical, including photocopy, recording, or any information storage and retrieval system, without permission in writing from the copyright owner. Your support of the author's right is appreciated.

Unless otherwise noted, all biblical references used are from the New Living Translation (NLT) ©

Published by VIA Consulting, LLC
Editor Sharenda Williams

Pastor Sabra has a unique anointing to help unlock your potential related to your life's purpose. Her ministry has profoundly touched and changed me. Her transparency is empowering and encouraging. Get ready to experience the transformative power of God as you read *unmask: Full Circle*.

Kathy Jordan, Sabra's Sister & Friend

In *unmask: Full Circle,* you will be pushed out of your comfort zone and into purpose. Pastor Sabra invites you into her past, detailing her most private and painful moments. Her transparency is encouraging and tangible as she details her process of overcoming shame, abuse, and self-doubt to become the mighty woman of God she is today.

Pastor Shawna Windham-Murray,
Ministry Assistant

Joining Sabra's Sisters has been a time of healing, learning, and bonding with other women. Pastor Sabra's teachings are presented with compassion and transparency. She has significantly impacted my life, and after reading *unmask: Full Circle,* you will be changed by her story as well.

Carole Lindsey, Sabra's Sister Mentee

Pastor Sabra's powerful teachings help you find strength and courage. As a mentor and author, she inspires you to wipe your tears, overcome the demons of your past, and conquer fears.
              Debra Harper, Sabra's Sister

What an amazing story of healing and transformation! You will feel God's power when you read unmask: Full Circle. It is real, raw, and non-religious. Pastor Sabra will inspire you to remove the mask and live the life God designed for you.
              Pastor Jaylan Windham-Murray,
                         Chapel Jonesboro

Overcomer! Pastor Sabra is all of that and more. We have all gone through tough seasons, but her story is uniquely distinct yet relatable. It is rare to find women in ministry willing to unmask their vulnerabilities to advance the lives of others. From the moment we connected, she has shown me genuine love and authentic grace. I am beyond excited about her first book, *unmask: Full Circle.* You will never be the same after reading this book.
              Renee Harrison,
                  Worship Leader & Friend

statement of purpose

I was created to worship God almighty through a lifestyle that embodies Christ's very nature, to develop and empower women to become what God has called them to be, and to help them fulfill their destiny in Him.

table of contents

dedication ---------------------------- 9

forward ------------------------------ 11

introduction -------------------------- 15

unmask ------------------------------ 23

marriage & ministry --------------- 39

truth & lies ------------------------- 53

pain & forgiveness --------------- 67

rejected & accepted ------------- 77

redesigned & reintroduced ------- 89

hell & heal -------------------------- 101

full circle ---------------------------- 113

dedication

To the one who I am ONE with,
My beloved husband, Donnie Skidmore.
You stood by me through the healing process,
and I am grateful that I get to stand by you
for the rest of our lives. Your faith moves mountains,
and your unconditional love for our family grounds me.
You became a father to our daughter Lindsey,
giving us both your last name and making us one family.
With our three sons and five grandsons,
we became the powerful family we are today.
I will love you forever. Because of you,
I can write this book with the confidence
that I have been completely restored.
Our best is yet to come!

forward

"You intended to harm me, but God intended it all for good. He brought me to this position so I could save the lives of many people."
(Genesis 50:20, NLT)

My mother is my best friend; her story has inspired me to never give up on God's plan. Her story is one of survival, hope, and healing. She is a woman of great courage who has overcome so much to write this book to encourage your life journey.

I am blessed to have walked this journey with my mother and witnessed the miracle of her full circle moment. Every time, the enemy thought he would get the victory with his plots and schemes to destroy her, But God! There was never a time God did not step in and clear the path for mother and me to witness his never-ending love. He was our protection and provision.

There were times of weariness when the will to keep going was fading. Life seemed hopeless, and the pain was never-ending. Yet, my mother kept the faith, never giving up on what God said, even when the pain of persistence was so great. Although stopping looked more pleasant, she never quit, and every step has led us to this place.

The book you are reading today is the result of Jesus Christ's finished work at Calvary. Much like our Savior, my mother was counted out and seemed to have no future. It looked like all hope was

forward

lost until the grave was found empty, and the world was forever changed. She is not just another woman in ministry; my mother is a world changer, taking others with her.

It has been said that hurt people hurt people, but the antithesis of that statement is that healed people heal people. Mother has been wounded, but that was not the end of her story. She allowed God to do what He does: heal. Now, she is on assignment to lead others to the Healer.

The pain that was supposed to silence her and keep her bound is now worn like a badge of honor. Her testimony confirms God is real and true. She reminds us that we have a purpose to fulfill as long as we are alive. It is my privilege to continue this journey with my mother. Not all steps will be easy or painless; distractions and detours will attempt to disrupt the ministry. However, just as Ruth refused to leave Naomi, so will I.

To my mother, you have always been my greatest advocate, and now it is my opportunity to do the same for you. My words are not enough to express my heart and how much your love, life, and survival have meant to me and will mean to many others.
I love you. I honor you. I celebrate you. You have come FULL CIRCLE!

Your daughter,
Lindsey Holbrook

· FULL CIRCLE · FULL CIRCLE ·

*I will praise thee:
for I am fearfully and
wonderfully made:
(Psalm 139:14, KJV)*

introduction

God created each one of us fearfully and wonderfully. However, the enemy will do everything in his power to prevent us from living the life God has planned for us. Insecurities, emotional bondage, relationships, and religion are some of the tools he will use to keep us from fulfilling our God-given purpose. Knowledge is power, and when we know what God has said about us, we can stand against anything the enemy tries to use to destroy us and our purpose.

As a young girl, I knew I was destined to do great things in the Kingdom of God. I knew that God wanted to use me to bring glory to His name, yet I still lacked confidence that I would be able to do and be everything that was expected of me. In my mind, I always wondered if I was enough.

At some point in life, everyone will likely feel insecure. Some may feel insecure about their outward appearance, weight, or shape, while others may experience an uncertain feeling that they are not worthy of love. This feeling will lead to difficulties in our relationships, including the most essential love relationship with God, the Father, and the Holy Spirit.

Overcoming insecurity starts with acknowledging its existence and affirming our identity in Jesus Christ by recognizing and identifying who God is in our lives and our need for Him in every area

introduction

of life. This will lead to embracing our own identity. If we cannot accept and embrace who we are and who God has created us to be, we may struggle to trust others in our lives.

While in prison, Paul encouraged the Philippian church and the reader today with his confident profession and confession of faith in God: *"For I can do everything through Christ, who gives me strength" (Philippians 4:13).* I dare you to have the same confidence in declaring these words over yourself, even in an uncomfortable situation.

Paul's words encouraged me as a child. Today, his words remain relevant as I pursue God's will. The confident woman writing this book, willing to reveal her deepest and darkest secrets, can only do so with the strength given to me by Christ. In my weakness, His strength perfects or matures within me. God's grace completes me when I feel less than enough.

Full circle is often used metaphorically to describe developments or changes. It also suggests that things have returned to their original form or condition. My story of coming full circle has not been easy, comfortable, or popular. It was a journey I had to take by myself while knowing I was not alone. Although Donnie is an amazing husband to me, father, grandfather, pastor, brother, and friend to many, he could not do this for me.

introduction

Much like a caterpillar in a cocoon, I entered a dark and sticky place for a season, but eventually, when the process was complete, a beautiful butterfly emerged. I had to confront my inner self and deal with my issues. This made removing the mask of shame, fear, insecurity, and bitterness easier. Without doing the work of inner healing, surrendering my will to God's will, and submitting to His voice, you wouldn't be reading this book. Let me say you would not have purchased it for spiritual reasons. It would have been a Sabra tell-all for the destruction of my enemies. What you are reading is not just my story but a true testament to the healing power of Jesus Christ in the life of a woman who had been betrayed, abused, and rejected. Here I am. I have emerged. I am no longer living in fear of rejection, the fear of my past, or the fear of my future. The masks have been removed, and I am free.

Ministry is my vocation, but it is more than a job or career. It is in my genetic makeup. My father was a pastor, and we worshiped in a large Pentecostal denomination. The strict rules often left families like ours having to choose between the organization or your family. Please do not hear what I am not saying; my daddy was a great man of faith; he was my best friend and mentor. However, when I went through my divorce, he was forced to remove me from serving. These seeds of rejection and feeling unworthy were planted in my heart for many years.

introduction

My greatest enemy was my memories. How could God ever use me after all the scandals, the divorce, and being a single mom? My heart was broken, and rejection had been the response of so many friends and loved ones. There was no way God was going to use this messy mess of a woman to lead a generation of men and women out of the bondage of their past and into the purpose of their future. But God!

Today, my tears of doubt have become tears of confidence and joy. God has restored me to lead others to restoration. First, I had to face my fear of rejection and become bold and courageous. Rejection and insecurity are the enemy's tactics to keep you from your divine assignment. Second, I had to be willing to remove the masks and live a life on full display. Removing your mask will require great courage. Shame is no longer my companion because I have been set free. I am submitting my will to His divine purpose and the perfect will of God.

Know that God is with you and will never leave you alone to become *"the you"* God ordained. He has big plans for your future, and God will equip you to accomplish them. *"For I know the plans I have for you," says the Lord. "They are plans for good and not for disaster, to give you a future and a hope." (Jeremiah 29:11).*

Your purpose is always connected to your most significant area of pain. This is not just a rote and religious cliché but a proven fact. I survived an abusive marriage, walked through a painful divorce, and

introduction

overcame rejection from those whom I loved the most. Now, I pastor a thriving church alongside my husband and mentor women worldwide.

At the time, I did not understand and often asked God, "Why me"? I mean, of all the sheltered daddy's girls, you chose me for a life of chaos. I wouldn't say I liked it then, but I appreciate it now.

In the kingdom of God, every loss is accompanied by a lesson. Armed with this knowledge, I have learned how to use every situation to the advantage of my divine assignment, the ministry of reconciliation.

You are reading this book because, as Paul wrote in Romans 8:28, "He is working all things together for my good." Incidentally, my things also work for you because God never wastes and has not wasted anything I have endured or experienced.

There is nothing you have done, will do, or that has been done to you that is too great for God to heal, forgive, and use for His glory. The death of Jesus abolished the shame of sin. We have been invited and authorized to go boldly to the throne of grace. In that invitation, there is strength and courage to do hard things like face the trauma of your past with an enduring faith in your future.

I am privileged to share my story with you, and I pray that God will use it to help you overcome what has seemingly been winning over you. I pray that the words of my testimony and the blood of the

introduction

lamb will shift the trajectory of your life and move you into a place of purpose designed by God just for you. As you read this book, I pray that you find the courage to shed your masks and emerge from your cocoon, embracing your purpose on earth.

This book is not one of those pretty stories with a magical ending. The details are gruesome, and only by the grace of God and His never-ending love can I fully share them with you. That was my disclaimer, so keep reading at your own risk.

If you are not ready for truth in love and to learn of God's supernatural power, close the book and return when you are.

If you are ready, let's get started!

It is your time.

Come Full Circle and Unmask!

FULL CIRCLE

I see you

I got you

~God

unmask

The beginning of my story was idyllic. I was raised in a pastor's home and expected to be like my father. Church attendance and service were not just a requirement but the standard. Daddy and I spent hours together visiting nursing homes and hospitals. He taught me how to love people and serve them humbly and faithfully. These times we shared were some of the best days of my youth. I respected him so much then and am grateful today for his leadership in our home. His willingness to spend this time with me personifies scripture.

> *"Train up a child in the way (s)he should go: and when (s)he is old, (s)he will not depart from it" (Proverbs 22:6, KJV, emphasis added)*

Outreach was one of the many lessons Daddy taught me. Perhaps the most valuable lesson was having a personal and thriving relationship with the Lord. He not only told me how to do it but also displayed it.

Looking back at the choices that created my life's rough and challenging circumstances, I am beyond grateful for the solid foundation that Daddy gave me. Only God knew what was to come in my life and how much I would need every lesson. Daddy always encouraged and mentored me to be the woman of God I was destined to become. I depended upon his guidance but eventually had to become responsible for my growth and maturity. I only sometimes got it right and probably got it wrong more often than I would like to confess. But this was the story God was giving me to share with you.

then & now

Our courtship was unusual and required some sneaking around. We met at a school chorus practice. He was in the chorus, and I was recruited to play piano for an upcoming concert. Our friendship was instant, and we spent time together outside of chorus practice. He was a senior, and I was a sophomore. To say I was flattered to get his attention would be an understatement. He knew all the right things to say to a sixteen-year-old sheltered daddy's girl. I quickly developed an attraction and romantic feelings for him.

We did not attend the same church, so I knew this relationship was dead. Although we shared many similarities, our differences would create an issue with my protective parents. The more we talked, the more we wanted to keep talking.

Our conversations were long and covered various topics, mostly about our faiths. He was a Nazarene, and I was Pentecostal. As I said before, it was a dead end, but we continued our relationship for some reason. No one in my family knew about him because my daddy would not allow us to date, so I minimized our hidden relationship to chats before and after school.

unmask

This single act of rebellion would be the catalyst for many years of devastating pain and heartbreak. Now, I know it was a setup by the enemy to cancel God's purpose. His scheme worked for a season, but trouble does not always last.

The enemy had a plan, but God's plan prevailed. What he planned to break me has made me stronger. What tried to silence me has made me much louder. Fear and shame have no place in my life. When they try to re-enter, I remember what my dad taught me, and I fight with the word of God.

the cover-up

In Genesis, God created heaven, earth, and man and gave him dominion over all creation. Humanity was to exist in the presence of God without shame or fear. Both males and females were naked. According to scripture, they were not ashamed.

However, after encountering a garden snake, disobedience or sin enters the perfect euphoric world God created for humanity to exist within. Suddenly, it was all disrupted, and their eyes were open to see their nakedness. It was not their nakedness that made them ashamed. It was their sin that made them cover themselves and hide from God. You and I were born naked and unaware of biases in the world. As we age, we become more aware of the nakedness.

unmask

When you become a certain age, no matter your gender, being uncovered is socially unacceptable in private or public. We learn to cover not only the necessary parts but the parts that should not be covered.

the masks

Masks cover your face, but metaphorically, they hide our true identities. They hide scars, bruises, broken hearts, black eyes, and whatever else you might be ashamed of for others to see. It might be fun to wear masks to a masquerade, but what about when the party is over, and you are still wearing them?

Masks hide your identity from others; over time, they will begin to hide it from you, which is where we have an actual problem. If masks were labels, most of us would be wearing multiple layers of masks. I have known people, me included, who have put on masks for temporary purposes and will put on another and another instead of removing the first mask. It becomes a cycle of covering up until they no longer know who they are.

Removing it is an act of courage, especially if you have worn it for a long time. Finding the confidence to be vulnerable with yourself is hard, and having the confidence to be vulnerable with others takes discernment and wisdom. God is ready when you are ready to peel off the masks. He has promised never to leave you or forsake you. His

unmask

love goes beyond your attempts to hide your truth. I once heard it said that people hate you on speculation, but God loves you with the evidence.

Have you ever told someone something from your past, and they looked at you like there is no way you experienced all that? They might have said, "I would not have ever thought or known by looking at you." Thank God I do not look like what I have been through.

There are two reasons why that statement is true. The first is because you are wearing a mask that portrays you as having no past, and you want all onlookers to see you as this well-put-together person. The second is where God wants us, unmasked and full circle. It is where we are willing to allow God to minister to our spirit and heal our brokenness.

We have removed the mask in private to experience a supernatural encounter with the Savior. Public unmasking is not always necessary. However, God will do what is needed to save you from yourself. If that means ripping off the mask in public, then that is what He will do.

He desires that no one perishes but that we succeed in Jesus Christ. Taking off the mask will take work. Living without the comfort of a mask will not be easy either. But I promise you will find the freedom of living unmasked much better than the masked bondage.

unmask

The weight of the masks becomes too much to carry, yet we continue to wear them and, when deemed necessary, add more. I can only imagine what I must have looked like wearing all those masks. Eventually, your face will get heavy. I suppose this is where the spirit of anxiety and depression is born. Anxiety is a fear of facing the truth of your reality that is beyond your control.

The Bible prescribes, "Be anxious for nothing but in all things by prayer and supplication." He instructs us not to be anxious and then specifies the resolution for not being anxious. Anxiety and depression are the fruit of prayerlessness and an unwillingness to release our issues to God daily. Anxiety is a choice we make, and prayer is the antidote. Paul urges you *to pray without ceasing (I Thessalonians 5:17, KJV)* and *give all your worries and cares to God, for he cares for you. (1 Peter 5:7, NLT).*

layers of labels

In this book, the term mask often refers to the invisible labels I have worn for many years. These labels include shame, fear, rejection, abuse, divorce, and so much more. I am a girl who loves labels, but they will not define me. Labels prevented me from living my best life according to God's purpose and plan.

One chapter of my life had defined everything, but I realized it was time lost. So many of you can relate to my story, while others will

unmask

struggle with its harsh reality. In another chapter, we will talk more about the lies that the enemy will tell you to keep you from the life that God planned for you before you were in your mother's womb.

His agenda is to keep you from your assignment. However, Paul writes that God will use all things to work for your good. It doesn't matter the enemy's tactics; you will win. The fight has been fixed in your favor. It might not look like it right now, but you are the winner because you serve the undefeated champion.

God will turn your ashes into beauty. This is more than words on a page; it is the truth. I am a living testimony of what God can and will do when you decide to cast your care upon Him. Give him every label, every hurt, every pain, every betrayal, and every heartbreak. Just as the Father waited for the prodigal son to return home, so does the Heavenly Father wait for you. His faithfulness to us is immeasurable and unmatched. No one can love us like he wants to, can, or will. Will you let him?

Self-imposed labels will keep you in bondage and from experiencing the greatest love of all time. God's agape or unconditional love will cover you on the journey to live a life of purpose. You are not what happened to you or what you have done. Yes, you have failed and will do so again and again. That, however, does not make you a failure.

unmask

just another label

When my marriage fell apart, I was ashamed and devastated without people's opinions. My family, friends, and the denomination I had faithfully served criticized and eventually ostracized me.

The divorce made me someone's ex-wife. It was like a sudden depreciation of my value. I was no longer allowed to play music at church. The religion did not approve of divorce and would seek to remove people from their positions of leadership. The people who attended our wedding and lauded our nuptials were now moving against me and requesting my immediate dismissal. Their behaviors and attitudes towards me were painful.

Post-divorce, I returned to my daddy's church, hoping to find love and support. Instead, friends turned their backs on me, blaming me for my husband's behavior. How is that even possible? Who encourages their husband to live a closeted gay life? Even though my conscious mind knew it was untrue, my bruised and broken heart was willing to accept the blame and the label.

For so many years, I carried the pain of his choices as if they were my own. I became cold and overtaken by all the hurt I had endured, not just by my husband but by other people as well. Hearing people admit they knew about my husband's sexuality was the most painful of all.

unmask

Driven by my anger, I did what any victim would do: I embraced the identity and then replicated the behavior. On a mission to wreak havoc, I got involved in a relationship that would destroy a valuable friendship. I was fully aware of the consequences of my actions, but *hurt people, hurt people.*

I was drowning in despair from the end of my marriage, loss of friendships, and being rejected by the church people. My sister was my constant, but I still felt alone. However, I realized that God never left Lindsey and me. We were always protected and provided for during this season.

Despite that, I continued to maintain my masks and labels, as the embarrassment of my past was too much to bear. I just wanted to keep moving forward and not think about or deal with the memories of my past. I feared that if people heard my story, they would alienate me, just like it had already happened.

beautiful disaster

God created the heavens and the earth in seven days and then rested. I married, honeymooned, graduated, and then led a revival with my new husband. While my classmates were planning senior trips and cruises, I was planning a wedding and becoming someone's wife. At seventeen, one week before my high school graduation, I walked down the aisle and married my best friend. We were young and in love, and we believed we were perfect for each other and would become a ministry power couple.

The wedding was beautiful and exceeded all my expectations. It was, without a doubt, the happiest day of my life. The church was packed with people from all over the state and within the church denomination. I was amazed and deeply grateful for their support.

We both knew that we would need their guidance and love as we embarked on this new journey of marriage. Seeing so many people gathered on that day was incredibly encouraging, and I felt confident that God had brought me and my best friend together on this path. I was on cloud nine, supremely unaware that my husband was keeping a secret that would change our relationship instantly and forever.

We traveled to a nearby town for our honeymoon. Once we arrived, we got some food and spent some time in the hot tub. Everything was going as I had hoped when he looked at me and said, "There is something I need to tell you. If we are going to have an honest relationship, there is something you need to know."

As he spoke, the next few moments felt like an eternity. He confessed to being in a sexual relationship and loving a man.

Unbelievable! Had I heard him correctly?

unmask

No longer feeling the joy and excitement of our wedding day, I was shocked and confused. Questions began to flood my mind, and I asked as quickly as I thought of them.

"Do you still love him?

"Are you saying you don't want to be married?"

"Does this mean you are gay?"

He insisted that he was not and wanted to move forward with the life we had planned.

Devastated and overcome with emotions, tears streamed down my face. I tried to understand what I had just heard. I ran into the bathroom, locked the door, and sat on the floor crying, praying for God's help. None of this was making any sense to me.

Why did he not tell me before now?

How do I live with and accept this truth?

Would I be able to stay married?

How did we get on our honeymoon, contemplating divorce?

And ministry? What about our ministry?

If we choose to divorce, the denomination could terminate our membership, and our plans for evangelism would be over.

What would I do?

If we would move forward and stay married, I wanted to know all the facts. I needed answers only he could give me. Finally leaving the bathroom, I sat on the bed and asked him to tell me everything.

unmask

He admitted to having more sexual relationships with other men but was not in love with them. Attempting to explain and make sense of his indiscretions, he revealed a childhood trauma. As a young boy, a neighbor molested him. He felt that experience was what led to his attraction to men.

My heart broke for him, and his vulnerability moved me as I listened to him share and tell me things he had never expressed to me or anyone else. I considered that he had become a victim of circumstances beyond his control and not his choice to be and do the things he had done.

After we prayed together, he promised it would never happen again and asked me to trust him. "I will try," I replied honestly.

As a daddy's girl, I lived a sheltered life, but as a preacher's kid, I was familiar with casting out demons. However, the evil spirits introduced and unleashed in our marriage that day were all new to me, and I was unprepared to deal with them.

When I share this part of my story, many people ask me, "Girl, why did you stay with him? You should have run then."

At that moment, it seemed simple: I loved him. However, in hindsight, I was possibly more in love with and attached to the beautiful life we had planned. Also, the fear of losing our dream life was more shameful than dealing with and facing reality. That night, I

unmask

chose to trust him, believing he would never betray me again, forgiving him, and remaining in the marriage.

We all had plans, but they were all different. My plans were to get married and fulfill God's call. Even though my husband seemed to want the same, he struggled with his own truth and desires. Of course, God's plan rivaled all of our plans. In His omniscience, God knew the end before the beginning. He knew I would stay in the marriage, face challenges, and even try to hide the truth. He planned to use it all for my good and His glory.

It is incredible how something designed to be beautiful can become a disaster. Our decision would become a beautiful disaster. Not his plan, not my dream, but God's will.

life provides

you with a cup,

you choose

how to fill it

-Sabra

FULL CIRCLE

marriage & ministry

Being a young bride presented its challenges. Like any girl my age, I had grand illusions about my desired life. I was looking for the "as seen on TV" life. All I ever wanted was to be a great wife to my husband and to do ministry as a couple. That was my fairytale, and I thought I had found it.

meet the parents, meet the pastors

Somewhat enjoying my rebellion, I was surprised when he showed up at our church on a Sunday night. He was on the precipice of ruining a good thing by coming here. How did he know where to find our church? I tried to remember but could not recall telling him where our church was. I had to stop thinking and act quickly before someone else got to him and exposed our secret friendship.

After greeting him, I introduced him to a few church people and my parents. I was nervous and afraid of how they would react to meeting him. Surprisingly, they were receptive to him. He and Daddy talked for a while before the service started.

He and I were from two different religious backgrounds, I knew the excitement was just getting started. A Pentecostal Sunday night could get wild and frighten the average churchgoer. I was sure

marriage & ministry

this would scare him away, but instead, he was hungry for more of the experience.

Afterward, he was invited to dinner with our family and church members. During the meal, he talked about the Nazarene church he and his family attended and had preached there several times. Just before leaving, he shared a cassette tape with Daddy.

Once the initial shock of the night had subsided, I was smitten by him and his enthusiasm for ministry. He never ceased to amaze me. First, showing up that night and then willingly embracing the Pentecostal experience, I knew he was the one for me. All things were working together for my good. God gave me exactly what I had prayed for a life and ministry partner. He and Daddy became close. It was a relief to no longer keep our friendship a secret and feel like a rebellious daughter.

Quickly, our relationship evolved from secret friends to an exposed couple of teenagers in love and planning a wedding. We had a momentous first year together. He graduated high school, and I started my junior year. Eventually, he joined the denomination and started evangelizing full-time. We planned to get married after I graduated from high school and then evangelize together. My senior year began, and so did the wedding planning.

With so many activities and plans, from preparing to graduate to finalizing wedding details, time moved fast. I wanted our

marriage & ministry

ceremony to be indicative of our future. Although anxious, I was also excited and hopeful for the journey we were about to begin. Finally, on Saturday, May 26, 1984, we were married.

good God, bad idea

After returning from our honeymoon, we rented a small house, and we were okay for the first six months, but the growing pains would come. Spending most of our time traveling for ministry, we led revivals that changed people's lives, later pastored a thriving church, and eventually had a beautiful daughter. Despite our perfect public image, we were living in a private hell. Thankfully, I would get out before our daughter would understand or experience the disaster.

Even as a young wife, I knew marriage would come with challenges. Therefore, the covenant vow between man and woman would require God. I learned that not all marriages are identical, and the movies lied. The happy ending I had planned, hoped for, and expected was far from what I would get. My decision to remain married meant putting away my childish expectations of the perfect mate and no longer living in an imaginary world.

He and I never spoke again about his honeymoon confession. I wanted to forget it, but I was haunted by the memory of the happiest day becoming the worst night. I loved my husband, but we were in big trouble. I prayed incessantly for him and the success of our

marriage & ministry

marriage. I thought we were doing okay, even during the tough times. Despite all our problems, we both chose to keep trying.

I would tell myself, "Ignore, ignore. It will get better, and we will be the couple everyone thinks we are."

Except my husband was keeping secrets and lying.

While doing laundry, I noticed an unfamiliar file cabinet. As I approached the mysterious cabinet, I felt sick in my stomach. I opened a drawer and found stacks of gay pornography. Betrayed a second time, I felt broken. At that moment, what I wanted to do, what I should have done, and what I did were different. I ran to my husband, yelling and crying. Again, he swore that he was not gay.

"It is the devil trying to break up our marriage," he said.

We built a fire and burned everything. If only that had been the final deception and the resolution to the problems in our marriage, my story may have had a different outcome. However, in retrospect, that day marked the beginning of the end of our marriage.

He started disappearing for an entire day and sometimes not coming home at night. When I questioned where he had been, he always said he needed time to seek God alone. I knew he was not being truthful, but it was often easier to accept what he told me rather than probe him for the truth.

In these moments, I would cry and beg God to tell me what I should do to help him to change. There was absolutely nothing I

marriage & ministry

could do for him. He would need to seek God and change his mindset. We often take our problems out of the hands of the problem solver. Let me encourage you to leave it in the hands of the man with the power to do all things. I was trying to do what only God can.

The next few years were heartbreaking rollercoasters of emotions. We would go to bed at night, and he would tell me how much he loved and appreciated me. Then, the following day, he confessed that he was still in love with the man he had a relationship with before me. He would wake me up in the middle of the night, admitting his indiscretions and asking for forgiveness.

With no one to confide in, I hid the truth from everyone. He would use scriptures to condemn me into staying if I threatened to leave. Later, I understood that this was the spirit of manipulation.

I continued to pray for him, and he often prayed all night, begging God to deliver him from the desire to be with men. I genuinely believe he wanted deliverance. But it requires a daily decision, intentionality, and a repentant heart.

God has given us all the freedom of choice, but every choice has its consequences. It would be easy to blame him for all our problems, but it would also be unfair. I chose to stay, hide the reality, and accept his behavior. From the moment he exposed the truth until the day I left, I identified as his victim. I realized that I was the victim of my choices. That is no longer my story, and it does not have to be

marriage & ministry

yours. While freedom is a choice, so is bondage. Perhaps you lack the strength or courage to escape your bondage. Let me encourage you with the Word of God.

"In my distress I prayed to the Lord, the Lord answered me and set me free". (Psalm 118:5)

Freedom is not just a choice but the birthright of the born again. Christ has set you free.

"If the Son therefore shall make you free, ye shall be free indeed." (John 8:36, KJV)

In the Greek, indeed is defined as *really, truly*. It is also related to the Greek word translated *"to be" or "I am."* You can declare, "I am really, truly free." The current situation might not match the declaration, but freedom is coming. The shed blood of the lamb did not just purchase your freedom, but it came with a lifetime warranty backed by the name of Jesus and guaranteed by God.

"For when God made promise to Abraham, because he could swear by no greater, he sware by himself." (Hebrews 6:13, KJV)

When you have been set free, stay free. Do not find yourself bound by the shame of your past or the uncertainty of your future. Live in your freedom today and every day.

"Stand fast therefore in the liberty wherewith Christ hath made us free and be not entangled again with the yoke of bondage." (Galatians 5:1, KJV)

marriage & ministry

blissfully toxic

Growing up a preacher's kid gives you the view from the top and the unrated knowledge of what can happen behind closed doors before your favorite preacher takes the pulpit. They had all the charisma but lacked character. I have known great preachers and pastors who had affairs, neglected their families, and embezzled church funds.

So many women silently tolerated what was happening right in front of them. Trying to protect the ministry and my daddy's legacy, I became one of them. I was happy to be married but not in a happy marriage. I loved him but hated the way he behaved and treated me privately.

Anguished by my weakness, I accepted his apologies and believed his promise never to do it again. My forgiveness became a free pass for him to go and do whatever with whomever. Our lives became a paradox of love and war. We had some great days, and then suddenly, all hell would break loose in our home. It was one day good and three days bad, two months of peace and four months of discord. I could not figure out what I was doing wrong and just wanted to find a way to improve things.

He admitted that he did not love me and that our marriage was a way to hide his attraction to men. His words pierced like a knife. He would often apologize for not loving me the way I should be loved, but the damage was done, and the apology did not take away the hurt of being unwanted.

We maintained a public image of a happily married couple but were both very unhappy. His desires constantly tormented him, and I wanted to be free from the lie we were living. It seemed like his temptations would overcome him as we tried to work towards a healthy marriage.

In April 1986, his sister, her husband, and their two-year-old child were all killed in a car accident. The grief was almost unbearable, but during that time, our marriage seemed to grow stronger. I hoped that as tragic as it was, God would somehow use this to turn things around for us. Everything went well for a while, but the same feelings and problems returned.

messy but real, real messy

I felt like my whole life would be lived lonely and unloved by a man who did not want to be with me. Then I found out that I was pregnant. We were excited, but I was even more excited because I thought, finally, someone who would love me.

My morning sickness was all day, and I did not get better until about five months into the pregnancy. However, we continued to travel, planning, and decorating the nursery in between engagements. We were preparing to start a weeklong revival locally

marriage & ministry

in Fayetteville, Georgia, so we would be home for a week. Things seemed to be going well and I was hopeful this baby would change the dynamics in our lives.

     Every moment of hope for our marriage was often coupled with an even more significant setback. I was getting ready for church one Sunday morning, and our home phone rang. I did not recognize the caller who asked to speak with me. It was a woman who was obviously very upset. After getting her name, she began to tell me about obscene phone calls that her husband had been receiving. They had a tracer put on the line and discovered that my husband had been making the phone calls. Before ending the call, she told me they fully intended to press charges. My heart was destroyed again.

This betrayal was different than the others because I was pregnant. If what she was saying were true, deep down, I knew it was; I was bringing an innocent child into a messy life. I confronted him with what this woman told me, and he denied it repeatedly. Assuring me the lady was lying, we went to church and ministered on Sunday morning and night.

"Please, God," I begged, "don't let this be real."

We were at my parent's house when my father told me the woman had been telling the truth. There were calls from our home phone and several from Daddy's church phone. He made the calls on a Wednesday night from the office while he was preparing to preach.

marriage & ministry

Now what?

Would they follow through with pressing charges, and if so, what did that mean for our child and me?

Hoping to resolve the matter without police involvement, a meeting was scheduled with the couple, with my father as mediator. We also discovered that this man was the brother of a close friend, and he pleaded our case to the couple. Thankfully, they agreed not to press charges if he never contacted them again. This was a huge relief for our family.

Evading criminal charges did not inspire change but made him worse. He no longer needed to hide the truth from me, meeting up with men regularly. Although my parents were privy to this occurrence, they had no idea how messy our lives had become.

this must be love

Love is a small word with immense ramifications. We all desire it, especially from the people closest to us. Limited knowledge of love can lead to unhealthy relationships or keep us attached past expiration. This was my testimony. Convinced this must be love, I remained in the marriage. Why? I loved him. He was my husband and the father of our daughter.

God has commanded husbands to love their wives as Christ loved the church and wives to submit to their husbands. Submission

marriage & ministry

is an organic reaction to being loved the right way. What must be examined is Jesus's love. When we understand how He loves His bride, we can know how we are to be loved as brides.

We were created by and for love, not to live in toxic and unhealthy relationships. Jesus's death restored the original intent to live in the presence and peace of God. We were living out of divine order. There was no peace or presence in our home because there was no "as Christ loved the church love" in our marriage.

Everything changed for me when Lindsey, our daughter, was born on December 8, 1988. She was perfect and became my lifeline. Her birth stirred the need for me to pull it together and find a way to create a safe and normal life for her.

Having a newborn meant staying home while he continued to travel and evangelize. His absence provided some peace, and I craved the permanence of that feeling. My love for our daughter gave me a new perspective. I needed to leave him and get out of our messy life. Unsure of when or how it would happen, God began ordering my steps and giving me divine instructions. It started with me getting a job and saving money.

FULL CIRCLE

your past does not disqualify you it prepares you

-Sabra

truth & lies

Our ministry was thriving and blessed beyond our wildest expectations. Every revival service was standing room only, with people flocking to hear the word of God and experience His presence. Yet, amid this success, our marriage was steadily disintegrating. The ministry kept us so busy that we barely had time for each other.

I often marveled at my husband's anointing, watching people come to know Jesus through his powerful sermons. However, behind the scenes, he was living a double life, and the conviction of his lies weighed me down.

We were not designed to carry the weight of our sins or the sins of others. Just as I could not do anything to make him better or change him, I was not responsible for carrying his convictions. Jesus was the mediator between life and death, sin and righteousness. His work at Calvary made Him responsible, not me.

If I only knew then what I know now.

There was an instance when he preached one of the best sermons I had ever heard at a small church. The congregation was deeply moved, with many responding to the altar call. As I bowed in shame, the weight of his deception pressed heavily upon me. I felt an overwhelming urge to expose him, tormented by the guilt of covering up his sin. The question that haunted me was, "How can this be?"

truth & lies

In that moment of despair, I heard God's voice softly but clearly: "Don't judge the message by the messenger." This revelation brought me an unexplainable peace. The questions, hurt, fear, doubt, and shame melted away for the first time in a long time. I felt safe. Desperate to save our marriage, I prayed fervently for my husband to have a transformative experience with God.

Denial had a firm grip on us both. It was not just the infidelity or the abuse that destroyed our marriage, but our unwillingness to define and deal with the root of our problems. Religion, with its rigid standards, didn't offer us the safety to be honest about our struggles. Even today, many confuse religion with the true church of Jesus Christ. The church should be a place of love and acceptance, where we reflect Jesus' welcoming nature. However, the institutionalized religion we experienced was harsh and unforgiving.

As the days turned into years, I became increasingly entrenched in denial. Every day I stayed in the marriage was another day I chose to ignore the truth. Denial does not make the problems disappear. It does, however, make you complicit in the lie. Living in denial is like living with the Cookie Monster, who denies taking the cookies despite the crumbs on his face.

truth & lies

deny, deny, denial

Denial is a powerful force, as destructive as any addiction. It allowed us to avoid the painful truths about our marriage and created a false sense of normalcy. For years, I lived a lie, presenting the façade of a perfect Pentecostal power couple while hiding the reality of our toxic relationship. Denial made it easier to stay, but it also trapped us in a cycle of abuse, infidelity, and compromise.

The ministry's success only amplified the dissonance between our public and private lives. My husband's charismatic sermons and public persona masked the private bully I faced at home. His confessions of infidelity, often with other men, were met with my misguided forgiveness, hoping each time it would be the last. This cycle of confession and forgiveness was exhausting, eroding my self-esteem and sense of worth.

Denial prevented us from addressing the root issues in our marriage. It wasn't just about the infidelity or abuse; it was about the deeper problems we refused to confront. We were both living in a false reality, unable to face the truth of our situation. Denial kept us from seeking the help we needed, both spiritually and psychologically.

Even within the church, denial was pervasive. Religion imposed impossible standards that left no room for honesty about our struggles. The fear of judgment and condemnation kept us silent, perpetuating the cycle of denial.

Living in denial took a heavy toll on my well-being. The constant stress and fear eroded my mental and physical health. I felt isolated and ashamed, trapped in a life that contradicted my faith and values. It wasn't until I began acknowledging the truth that I started to see a way out.

red flags

On our wedding day, I stood before God, our family, and friends, ready and willing to become a wife, fulfilling the vows, for better or worse, for richer or poorer, in sickness and in health until death do us part. Young, but not naïve to the possibility of problems and growing pains in a marriage. What I was not ready for was the verbal abuse and violent attacks.

There was never a clear indication of my husband's sexual deviance before his honeymoon confession. I did often wonder if his confession of the affair and the admission of childhood abuse was his way of excusing his behavior so that he could continue it. Nonetheless, the truth will set you free if you can accept it.

I was not only willing to stay in the marriage, but I committed to doing things to satisfy his needs and desires. Although I was willing to change for him, he was unwilling to do the same for me or himself. The imbalance in our commitment to the relationship was a red flag.

Despite being called red flags, they can often be challenging to see. Identifying a red flag requires that you know yourself, your expectations of the other person, and their capacity to follow through. Red flags should not only be searched for in others but also looked for in yourself. I had to come face to face with the woman in the mirror many times. It was both uncomfortable and not pretty.

There were several red flags in our marriage. As I mentioned, admitting his same-sex attraction and my preceding choice to stay in the marriage. Despite how I felt about his choices, he continued to see other men, and my acceptance of the behavior was a red flag. When he asked me to do things under the guise of the undefiled marriage bed to satisfy his desire and my compliance. The abuse, verbal and eventually physical, was also a red flag in our marriage.

Denial is a red flag in any relationship, whether a marriage, a friendship, a colleague, or a family member. I was the best at being in denial about the state of our marriage. When things would happen in our marriage, I did what I knew how to do: live in it and live with it.

the enemy lies

There are two truths we can always rely on. First, God does not lie. It is impossible and completely goes against His identity. Second, the devil is a liar. The Bible is very specific about this, calling him the father of lies.

According to John 10:10, The devil comes to kill, steal, and destroy. His agenda is to keep us away from the tailored purpose and future God designed before we were formed in our mother's womb. He will do anything to keep you distracted, hidden, or make you remain silent.

The good news is that he will not succeed in his attempts to kill, steal, or destroy you. Jesus has defeated the adversary, and we can live a victorious life, flaws and all. We will be met with challenges, but we have an advocate who defends and protects us, even from ourselves.

As you read this story, be encouraged that if God is for you, who can be against you? He is greater than any pain, problem, or person who will try to keep you from God's plans. As you pursue God and purpose, remember these three things.

1. The devil is a defeated liar.
2. You have the victory in Jesus.
3. The promises of God are everlasting.

we lie to ourselves and others

The enemy will lie to us, but that is who he is. Nothing he says compares to the lies you tell yourself. Before ever lying to another person, you will lie to you first. There are various reasons, such as

truth & lies

shame, pain avoidance, social convenience, and protection. Lying to you creates a false sense of security and optimism. There is only temporary relief in lying, but it can have long-term effects, such as preventing personal growth and self-awareness.

What might feel like protection becomes a mask and the subsequent loss of your identity. Your secret lies become a public truth. Although you are hurting, the mask prevents you from being seen. Lose the mindset that it is easier to live a lie than to face the truth. People will always judge your present without the knowledge of your past. Eventually, you no longer have to care about their thoughts and live according to your truth. Not only are you living in denial, but you are denying yourself the life God designed for you.

Every decision I made was centered around my love for him and the lie I was telling myself. Living in denial is not a commitment you should be willing to accept, but accepting the truth is the first step toward freedom. You were not created to live a lie.

After every indiscretion and decision to stay, I would say, "This is the last time." Oh, the lies we tell ourselves to protect us from dealing with the truth. He promised me it would be the last time and that it would never happen again. Every promise preceded another lie. Eventually, I had to stop lying to myself and others. When I decided to no longer participate in the lie called our marriage, I found joy and freedom. The truth set me free.

truth & lies

freedom from denial

While I was not the perfect wife, I was intentional about my role as a wife. Eventually, I accepted the truth about our marriage; I was not and never would be what he wanted. As a result, he became physically aggressive. In the beginning, I took his abuse, but near the end of the marriage, I started to fight back.

We had an intense argument about six months before moving into our final home together. My husband's anger escalated, and the verbal abuse became vicious. He pushed me down on the bed, restrained me, and, in a degrading act, blew bodily fluid onto my face and tried to rub it into my mouth.

This was the most humiliating experience of my life. I felt as though I was no better than the fluid that he was smearing all over me. The sudden recognition of my reality and that I was not enough for him or anyone else. I was finally starting to come out of the fog of denial. I was no longer willing to be his victim, so I began to fight.

Another change was on the horizon when we were approached with an offer to pastor a local church. The new salary and my job meant we could afford a larger home. We accepted the position, and there was a fresh excitement that I had not felt in a long time. Everyone at the church welcomed us; we found a new house and started planning community outreach. This was just what we needed: a new beginning and a fresh start.

truth & lies

Just as before, the good times did not last. An argument ensued, and he began saying some mean and hateful things to me. His words cut deep. Needing to clear my mind and regain my composure, I decided to retreat to our bedroom. Our daughter was asleep in her room, so I could be alone without distractions.

He decided to follow me and continued spewing vile and hateful words. The more he spoke, the angrier he became. He pushed to the bed and slapped. I jumped up from the bed, ready to engage in this fight, but before I could swing at him, he grabbed me and threw me, breaking the window. I tried running for the door, but he got there first, slamming the door and locking me inside.

This brutal confrontation made me realize that my life was in danger. My arm was injured, and it was my elbow that broke the window. Escaping this room meant getting out of this marriage. I considered climbing out the window, but our house had a full basement, so our bedroom was on the second floor. Instead, I sat weeping, waiting for him to calm down and unlock the door.

After about two hours, he calmed down and said he would unlock the door if I promised not to leave. I agreed to stay, but when he opened the door, I grabbed my keys and purse and ran to the van. It was pouring rain that night, but I drove away quickly. In my haste to leave, I left my daughter asleep in bed.

truth & lies

Maybe I instinctively knew she would be safe with him. His problem was with me. I was the one who made him miserable to the point of lashing out violently. My life was in danger, and the only way to truly protect my daughter was to survive. So, I drove to the hospital, where they did x-rays and then cleaned and stitched my wound.

I decided to call my sister and a friend. After leaving the hospital, I drove to my sister's, and my parents met me there. I gave my father the rundown of the evening events. He called my husband to inform him we were coming to get my daughter. It was about 2 a.m. when we arrived at the house. I packed a bag, got my baby girl, and told him the marriage was over.

Leaving my husband was the hardest decision I ever made, but it was also liberating and necessary for my survival. Despite the physical pain, the emotional relief was immense. Breaking free was not about leaving my husband but reclaiming my life and identity. It required facing the truth, seeking help, and making tough decisions.

Looking back, I see how denial kept me in bondage and how breaking free was the key to my healing. The road was not easy, and the scars are a reminder of the battles fought. But I also see the hand of God guiding me, providing strength and comfort. Healing is an ongoing process; each day is a step towards wholeness.

truth & lies

I moved in with my sister, consulted with an attorney, and began divorce proceedings. This marked the beginning of my journey towards freedom. The following months were challenging as I navigated the legal and emotional aftermath, but my faith sustained me. Though fraught with fear and uncertainty, each step brought me closer to freedom and healing. I leaned on God's promises, finding comfort in scriptures that spoke of His protection and provision.

Throughout this ordeal, my faith was both a lifeline and a source of inner conflict. On one hand, my relationship with God provided moments of peace and clarity. On the other hand, my denomination added to the pressure and guilt I felt and presented a different set of challenges. Divorce was considered a sin, and the stigma attached to it was significant. The fear of judgment from our religious community made deciding to leave even harder. Yet, I knew that staying in the marriage was causing more harm than good.

Ultimately, my faith in God's love and mercy gave me the courage to leave. I realized God wanted me to live free from denial and bondage. God's love and acceptance became my guiding principles, reminding me that regardless of my past or present struggles, He was always with me and for me. I often found solace in prayer, seeking God's guidance and strength.

This spiritual journey was not easy, but it was necessary. It taught me the importance of aligning my life with God's truth, even when it meant making difficult decisions. My faith provided the strength to break free from the mask of denial and to live a healthier, more honest life.

you are there to stay

The enemy was on an assignment to destroy me and my future. Unaware of how I was going to get out, I was stuck in a cycle of betrayal and denial. The enemy had me convinced that I was there to stay and that I would die there. But God!

In the final violent attack, I believe death was after me. If I had not survived, it would have impacted the life of my daughter, and the purpose God had for my life would have died with me. I was determined to live for me and my daughter. I was destined to lead women to acceptance, healing, and forgiveness.

The enemy said you will die here, but God said you will not die here, but you will live to declare My Word. Please do not allow the enemy to deceive you into believing his lies propagating death. Instead, remind him of what God has promised you, and tell him you are here to stay.

FULL CIRCLE

*do not wait for
feelings to change
forgive and then
feelings change*
-Sabra

pain & forgiveness

Pain often lurks as a silent yet potent force in the quiet corners of our hearts. For many, this pain stems from betrayal and brokenness, shaping our perspectives and influencing our paths. This chapter will delve into the transformative journey of pain, forgiveness, and purpose.

My husband's unfaithfulness and abuse led me into a spiral of pain and bitterness. After finding the courage to leave the toxic marriage, I embarked on a journey of healing and rediscovery. Pain can lead to profound personal growth and a deeper understanding of our purpose when met with faith and forgiveness. Embracing forgiveness and seeking divine guidance can transform our darkest moments into sources of strength and inspiration.

Forgiveness is a moral duty and a pathway to spiritual and emotional freedom in the Christian faith. Jean Vanier says, "Love is an act of endless forgiveness." However, forgiveness is often considered one of the most challenging yet profoundly liberating acts we can undertake. Many people struggle with it. In a dialogue with Peter, Jesus explains the boundless nature of forgiveness that we, as believers, must embody.

pain & forgiveness

Then Peter came to him and asked, "Lord, how often should I forgive someone who sins against me? Seven times?" "No, not even seven times," Jesus replied, "but seventy times seven!"
(Matthew 18:21-22)

Leaving the marriage was only the beginning of my path to healing. It was a pivotal step in my journey towards healing and rediscovery. I also had to forgive the man who had caused me so much pain and forgive myself for allowing him to do so repeatedly.

Let me also explain that forgiveness is not about condoning the wrong done to us but releasing others and ourselves from anger and bitterness. It is not about forgetting, and remembering is not an excuse not to forgive. Forgiveness can be challenging. Our ability to forgive is rooted in the grace and mercy we receive from God.

"Instead, be kind to each other, tenderhearted, forgiving one another, just as God through Christ has forgiven you." (Ephesians 4:32)

the bitterness of betrayal

Betrayal is a seed that will eventually harvest as bitterness. Betrayal is like a knife in the back, shattering trust and leaving a person vulnerable and alone. Hurtful, destructive, and cruel, the pain of betrayal penetrates to the core of your being.

The act of betrayal is out of your control, but becoming bitter is a choice. The circumstances of my marriage made me angry, and

pain & forgiveness

the constant betrayal turned to bitterness. Although my feelings were justified, staying there was not.

Overcoming bitterness was a daily decision. I realized that holding onto bitterness only chained me to the past and would prevent me from moving forward. The decision to heal meant exposing the root of my bitterness. If you do not deal with it, you will not heal.

In the Christian faith, bitterness is often left unaddressed. As believers, we wear our masks so well, pretending and never getting healed. I know this from personal experience. We both deserved an Academy Award for our public performances.

I remember thinking I would never get over him or the trauma of our marriage. Then I would question God, "Why me?" Maybe you are asking the same question. It has also been asked, "Why not you?" Then I think of the greatest betrayal of all time: Judas betrays Jesus. This shifts the trajectory of my thinking from questioning to gratitude.

The measure of my betrayal does not compare to what Jesus experienced, which would be a testament to His love for you and me. He could have thwarted the enemy's plan, but He saw through the cross to the other side, and *"Because of the joy awaiting him, he endured the cross, disregarding its shame."* (Hebrews 12:2).

pain & forgiveness

Bitterness has been categorized as a sin, but what if it is instead a sickness needing a healer? In John chapter five, Jesus encounters a lame man who has been in his condition for thirty-eight years. He asks him one question: *"Will you be made whole?"* The lame man responds, "I had no one to put me into the water." Jesus's rebuttal is simple but powerful: *"Take up your bed and walk."*

What if it were that simple to be free from the bitterness of betrayal? Well, I am telling you that it is. Jesus, our healer and savior, says to each of you, *"Take up your bed and walk."* How will you respond? Will you stay or get up?

from pain to purpose

Pain is an inevitable part of the human experience, but the potential for profound transformation and purpose lies within its depths. My pain would catalyze personal growth and a deeper connection to God. It is in that pain that my purpose was found.

It would be years before I would see the purpose in my pain. Just as I chose to trust my husband on our wedding night, I had to trust God has a purpose and a plan for my pain.

"For I know the plans I have for you," says the Lord. "They are plans for good and not for disaster, to give you a future and a hope."
(Jeremiah 29:11)

pain & forgiveness

My past was a series of unfortunate events and divine preparation for a future ministry. The pain was part of my story but not the whole story. My experiences equipped me with unique insights and empathy for those feeling battered and betrayed. Now, I can provide that safe space for women to share their stories, seek healing, and discover their purpose.

the blessing of forgiveness

It has been said that forgiveness is not for the other person but for you. That is the blessing of forgiveness. Forgiveness allows individuals to move forward without being anchored by past hurts. It liberates them from the negative impact of past experiences and enables them to embrace the future with a positive outlook.

The blessing of forgiveness lies in its ability to heal, restore, and uplift both the forgiver and the forgiven, contributing to a more fulfilling life. There are physical health benefits, spiritual well-being, and peace because of forgiveness. Although challenging, forgiving my ex-husband and those who contributed to my past hurts was my ticket to experiencing a life of freedom.

It would have been much easier for me to remain bitter and angry. However, it would have prevented me from having my life today—one filled with joy, peace, and so much love for myself. I can love my family better because I chose to forgive. I can also love those

pain & forgiveness

who despitefully use me because I know the blessing of forgiveness and the freedom that comes as a result.

True freedom in Christ begins with the understanding that God unconditionally loves and accepts us. This truth is the foundation for breaking free from the past. I had to unlearn the lies of being unworthy, unloved, and trapped. Instead, I clung to the truth of God's word, which reminded me of my worth and freedom being rooted in Christ, not the circumstances or opinions of others.

"So Christ has truly set us free. Now make sure that you stay free, and don't get tied up again in slavery to the law." (Galatians 5:1)

Freedom is a choice, a daily decision to live by faith. While I was writing this book, I was faced with the need to forgive again. I was not intentionally holding onto anything, but the emotions that flooded my mind while reliving this time required me to stop and say the words out loud. "I forgive you, and I forgive me."

Maybe there is someone you need to forgive. Perhaps you need to forgive yourself. Whatever it is, I encourage you to forgive. If you can't face them, write a letter or make a phone call. Seek wise counsel on the best way forward. Just do not refuse freedom and remain stuck.

pain & forgiveness

pack light

I love to travel, but most people dislike traveling with me. As the one loading and unloading my luggage, my husband becomes frustrated and complains about my tendency to overpack when we travel. I almost always pack for three weeks on a one-week trip. I need options because I do not know my mood when we arrive.

While this sounds comical, it is not funny and can be deadly in the spiritual. We were not designed to carry the weight of pain, the acts of betrayal, or the sickness of bitterness. Just as Jesus heals, he also wants to take our burdens. There is rest for the weary and brokenhearted.

> *"Then Jesus said, "Come to me, all you who are weary and carry heavy burdens, and I will give you rest. Take my yoke upon you. Let me teach, because I am humble and gentle at heart, and you will find rest for your souls. For my yoke is easy to bear, and the burden I give you is light." (Matthew 11:28-30)*

What are you carrying? Is it the weight of depression, shame, and anxiety? Maybe it is financial, marital, or your children? What you are holding will weigh you down and affect your mobility. You cannot move forward freely, which delays your journey to purpose. Eventually, you will stop moving and become stuck in a season that was only supposed to be temporary. You don't have to bear the weight of the world alone. Give it to God and rest, knowing He

pain & forgiveness

controls everything and will work everything for your good. Jesus says that we can cast all our burdens, the things that weigh us down, on Him because He loves and cares for us.

"Casting all your care upon him; for he cares for you." (1 Peter 5:7)

FULL CIRCLE

*pain can be fuel
if you use it wisely
-Sabra*

rejected & accepted

Rejection is a word that carries a weight most of us know all too well and comes in many forms. Whether it's a failed relationship, a job we didn't get, or a friendship that has drifted apart, rejection can feel like a personal assault on our worth. It leaves you questioning your value, abilities, and your very existence. The mask of rejection creates a narrative that something is wrong with me.

When you can shift your focus from seeking acceptance from people to finding it in God, rejection loses its power. Turning to God for acceptance does not negate our need for human relationships but reprioritizes a toxic relationship with a healthy one. Unlike human love, God's love is unwavering and unconditional.

"And I am convinced that nothing can ever separate us from God's love. Neither death nor life, neither angels nor demons, neither our fears for today nor our worries about tomorrow- not even the powers of hell can separate us from God's love. No power in the sky above or in the earth below- indeed, nothing in all creation will ever be able to separate us from the love of God that is revealed in Christ Jesus our Lord." (Romans 8:38-39)

the pain of rejection

After years of saying he loved me and then confessing to never loving me, rejection became the centerpiece of our relationship. My husband's desire for men led to a toxic cycle of being rejected and seeking acceptance. I so desperately wanted to be who and what he desired. Once I realized and accepted that I would never be that for him, the sting of rejection was even more significant.

However, his rejection would not be the only hurt I would experience. After our divorce, I returned to my daddy's church. Expecting to be met with love and compassion, I was rejected. Not only had I lost my marriage, but the religion that I had been a part of my entire life was lost to me also.

I knew my decision to dissolve our marriage would have consequences, but I had no idea the gravity of the collateral damage. The place where I should have been restored was now where I felt more broken. Already the victim of his lies, cheating, and abuse, I was now the casualty of a religion and church I loved.

Nevertheless, I prioritized providing a safe and stable environment for my daughter and me. The pain of rejection was almost unbearable at times. Feeling bitter, hopeless, and disconnected, I continued attending church.

the power of rejection

Some things happen to you, while others will happen for you. An example is Jesus's betrayal and rejection. The paradox of the story is that His rejection would lead to our redemption. The power of

rejected & accepted

rejection is freedom. Rejection isn't comfortable, but it is often necessary.

If there had been no betrayal, there would have been no cross. It was all required to get Jesus to Calvary for our salvation. Everything I experienced was a prerequisite to my purpose. I had to experience the rejection of my husband, my religion, my family, and my friends. Being the ostracized hot topic wasn't easy, but I survived it all just for you.

the protection of rejection

Recognize the protection of rejection as a divine redirection. It does not feel good and might be a blow to your self-esteem or a setback. My heart desired to be married and in ministry with my husband. At the end of our marriage, I focused on the immediate disappointment but later saw the future blessing God had for me.

"We can make our plans, but the Lord determines our steps"
(Proverbs 16:9)

Embracing rejection as divine protection allows you to navigate the hard times with resilience and trust, knowing that every opposition prepares you for God's plans. The Bible provides many examples of this divine redirection and protection. Joseph was sold into slavery by his brothers. Although they sought to get rid of him, God was repositioning Joseph to protect and provide for his family.

rejected & accepted

Moses raised an Egyptian and was rejected by the Egyptians. An accused murderer fled to the desert and had a burning bush experience. This rejection led him to his true calling as the leader who would free the Israelites from bondage.

David was rejected by his father, brothers, and Saul, but God had plans for the man after His own heart, anointing him king and returning him to the sheep pasture. Later, his father sent him on assignment to deliver food to his brothers, who were at war, and they mocked him instead of appreciating him for the delivery. David defeated Goliath, and Saul became jealous of his fame and conspired to kill David. All these things prepared David to be the leader he was destined to be.

When experiencing rejection, let these stories remind you of how God manipulates man's plans for your good. Trust that God is always working in the background on your behalf. You might not be able to see God's hand in your situation, but I can assure you that He is there.

As I inventory my life today, my relationship required rejection for me to know God beyond religion. Once I shifted my perspective on the pain of rejection, understood its power, and accepted its protection, I removed the mask and was able to see its purpose. I no longer feared the rejection of men but lived in the acceptance of God.

rejected & accepted

the value of acceptance

The opposite or full circle of rejection is acceptance. Acceptance contributes to our mental and emotional well-being. With God's acceptance, we experience less stress and anxiety, have healthier relationships, and live fulfilling lives.

True acceptance comes from within and knowing your value. People only reject what they do not value or cannot afford. Knowing who you are and to whom you belong is essential when measuring your value.

"I will praise thee; for I am fearfully and wonderfully made; Marvellous are thy works; And that my soul knoweth right well." (Psalms 139:14, KJV)

Fearfully means a reverent awe, and wonderfully means to be separated or distinct. You have been created with a distinction that requires reverence. To be fearfully and wonderfully made encompasses the original intent of God.

"Then God said, Let us make human beings in our image, to be like us…" (Genesis 1:26)

We can accept rejection as an appropriate response to what can't be explained or expressed. Acceptance acknowledges the distinguishing nature of our existence. We were not created to fit in but to stand out. God's acceptance demands the pain of rejection.

rejected & accepted

the victory of acceptance

I remember going to church camp and playing softball. I was always the last one chosen because I was not athletic. It was embarrassing and made me question whether I would be good enough. I knew my talents were not in athletics, but there was a joy in being chosen. These experiences can affect our self-esteem as adults and make us question who we are. I know that I am unique and vital to God, and He created me for a specific purpose, and I am okay with not being chosen for softball or anything else.

"For you are a holy people, who belong to the Lord your God. Of all the people on the earth, the Lord your God has chosen you to be his own special treasure." (Deuteronomy 7:6)

"Approval required" is the best way I can explain our religion. It was strict, but like most man-made idealogues, it lacked the most fundamental attribute of the Christian way: grace in love. Many preached it as a gift from God to us, but those who themselves had been recipients hardly ever displayed it.

Acceptance is a triumphant victory over self-doubt, fear, and rejection. My religion could not offer me the acceptance I desired. It would only come from God. God already chose and accepted me before He even formed the world.

"Even before he made the world, God loved us and chose us in Christ to be holy and without fault in his eyes." (Ephesians 1:4)

rejected & accepted

The victory of acceptance is overcoming obstacles that hinder our sense of self-worth and embracing our identity. The next time you feel overlooked and rejected, remember that God has chosen and accepted you. When you are faced with a fearful situation, remember God has equipped you to face and overcome your fears.

"For God has not given us a spirit of fear and timidity, but of power, love, and self-discipline." (2 Timothy 1:7)

the voice of acceptance

The affirmation of worth and existence comes from a gentle, reassuring whisper. It can come from an internal voice, an external voice, or the divine voice of God. Having a relationship with God is how you can hear and respond to the voice of acceptance. The voice says, "You are enough," "You are loved," and "You are worthy."

The internal voice is your self-talk. What are you saying to you about you? Your self-talk must have a foundation in the word of God if it will change your situation. Paul writes and encourages you to think of things that are true, noble, right, pure, lovely, and admirable.

"And now, dear brothers and sisters, one final thing. Fix your thoughts on what is true, and honorable, and right, and pure, and lovely, and admirable. Think about things that are excellent and worthy of praise." (Philippians 4:8)

The external voice of acceptance comes from affirmations from friends, family, and community members. It is imperative to

rejected & accepted

surround ourselves with people who uplift and support us. I am learning to surround myself with women who can speak life to me and those around them. God has anointed me to do the same with those I have a relationship with or encounter.

"Don't use foul or abusive language. Let everything you say be good and helpful, so that your words will be an encouragement to those who hear them." (Ephesians 4:29)

The words of those in your community will impact your internal voice. Again, surround yourself with people who will support your future and not diminish your existence. If I am encouraged by others, then encouraging myself will not be as difficult. I can repeat their words until I start believing what I hear.

"So then, let us aim for harmony in the church and try to build each other up." (Romans 14:19)

The same is true with the voice of God. The voice of God is the most important and profound of the three voices of acceptance. When you cannot speak to yourself or the people around you are silent, the voice of God is always speaking. If you cannot hear Him audibly, you can go to the Word of God. What God says about you in His Word is an unvarnished and unchanging truth.

"For we are God's masterpiece, He has created us anew in Christ Jesus, so we can do the good things he planned for us long ago." (Ephesians 2:10)

rejected & accepted

If you have the Word of God, you will always have God's voice to encourage you. God's acceptance does not eliminate man's rejection. However, his acceptance will empower you to overcome people's rejection. He chose you, flaws and all, making you holy and acceptable.

"But you are not like that, for you are a chosen people. You are royal priests, a holy nation, God's very own possession. As a result, you can show others the goodness of God, for he called you out of the darkness into his wonderful light." (1 Peter 2:9)

FULL CIRCLE

God will not let you quit in the valley
—Sabra

redesigned & reintroduced

Life is often unpredictable, filled with moments of joy and times of profound sorrow. Trauma and tragedy can leave us feeling broken, lost, and disconnected from our purpose. However, God offers a path to healing, transformation, and renewal in our deepest pain.

> *"The Lord is close to the brokenhearted; he rescues those whose spirits are crushed." (Psalms 34:18)*

Pain will shake your faith but is also a catalyst for spiritual growth. You have been learning about the broken me, but I want to shift the focus to the restored me. The marriage, the abuse, the divorce, and the rejection had stripped me of my identity. But God understands our pain and transforms us from the inside out. He was redesigning me emotionally, mentally, and spiritually so that He could reintroduce me to my purpose and all of those who tried to destroy me.

just a phase

If you have children, you can relate to the statement, "It's just a phase." I often tell my son and daughter this when their boys disobey or talk back. One day, my daughter said, "Everything is a phase to you. When will the phases be over?"

redesigned & reintroduced

If anyone knows my daughter, they can relate to why I found her question hilarious. Maybe it was the frustration in her voice or the truth of her statement. I laughed when she asked, and I am laughing now. The truth is that we all go through phases, some good and some bad.

"For everything there is a season, a time for every activity under heaven." (Ecclesiastes 3:1)

Just as my daughter asked when the phases would end, I had the same question when I was going through times of abandonment and loneliness. I believe you are asking God the same question. The end came when I decided enough was enough and pursued God and His guidance.

God is ready to give you a fresh start, but what are you doing to get it? Stay faithful to the word, commit to prayer, and seek God's will. Whatever phase or season you are in today, hold on and wait. Your change is on the way. It is just a phase.

"Weeping may last through the night, but joy comes with the morning." (Psalm 30:5)

the dressing room

I love to travel, and I love to shop before, during, and sometimes after. I wouldn't say I like the dressing room, but I understand their purpose. In the stores, customers can try on their items before purchasing. In life, we only sometimes get to try on what we get.

redesigned & reintroduced

However, because God is gracious, we can enter the dressing room of life to take off old garments and put on new clothes.

You have the right to change and to be changed. Just as clothes are seasonal, so are people, places, and pain. You do not have to stay in last season's clothes. If God has given you the grace to escape the grave, then He can give you the grace to change your garments! You can enter the dressing room to remove the old and put on the new.

"Now Joshua was clothed with filthy garments, and stood before the angel. And he answered and spake unto those that stood before him, saying, Take away the filthy garments from him. And unto him he said, Behold, I have caused thine iniquity to pass from thee, and I will clothe thee. With change of raiment." (Zechariah 3:3-4, KJV)

God heals from the inside out. He gives us the strength to confront and overcome our emotional burdens. Only God can heal your heart and bind your wounds.

"He heals the brokenhearted and bandages their wounds."
(Psalm 147:3)

He will heal you privately to present you publicly. However, it will require your participation. You must be willing to come to Him just as you are. If you are dressed out of season, you can end this phase with a change of clothes.

Do not concern yourself with those who are watching and judging. You know what you need from God, and He wants to give it to you. Do not be afraid to abandon your old garments, just as

redesigned & reintroduced

Lazarus with the grave clothes and Bartimaeus with his cloak did. They no longer needed their garments because Jesus changed their situations and identities.

Are you dressed for the occasion? Our clothes tell the story of who we are, where we have been, and where we are going. If your garments are too small, it's time to upgrade. If they are filthy, get them clean. If they are no longer your style, get what fits your identity best. It is time to dress for where God is taking you. Dress for success!

destined for greatness

As I settled into my new phase of life as a divorced single mom, I was sure God was not going to use me again in ministry. But God planned to use my greatest struggle to produce the most significant victories. I love how God uses every success and failure in our lives to show us His glory.

Despite my past, God ordered my steps, and I would be destined for greatness. To be destined means to be set apart for a particular purpose. Knowing your purpose and sowing into the lives of others is how you achieve greatness. Every moment of my life has been set up to set me apart for success.

The past will impact you in two ways: breakdowns or breakthroughs. There were many days I chose to break down, but

redesigned & reintroduced

God would not let me stay there. He was pushing me to experience breakthroughs.

In Jeremiah 29:11, God declares that we have an expected end. He set me apart for a purpose and would use that to bless others. You and sometimes people will put you in a box, label you, and cast you away. Although some labels lie, some are factual.

I was broken.
I was divorced.
I was rejected.
I was abandoned.

Before I was in my mother's womb, married, a parent, divorced, rejected, and ashamed, God called me His. Labels are not always the end; they can also be a new beginning. If you are wearing the labels of your past, enter the dressing room to experience a divine makeover. The perils of life will change you, but God wants to reintroduce you as He intended, in His image and after His likeness.

in his image

Understanding that we are made in God's image is a profound truth that can transform our lives, especially as we seek to recover from past pains and failures. Being made in His image confirms that we do have purpose and meaning. Embracing our identity in God equips us with the strength and perspective to heal and pursue that purpose.

redesigned & reintroduced

Of course, the enemy had other plans for me. He wanted to keep me stuck by silencing me, making me feel unworthy, and robbing me of the courage to share my story. Although he cannot rightly divide the word, the enemy knows our testimony will inspire and encourage those going through similar struggles. He knew if I were ever to start speaking and sharing my story, the lives of both men and women would be forever changed. Our testimony shows God's transformative power and brings hope to those who need encouragement.

> *"And they overcame him by the blood of the Lamb, and by the word of their testimony; they loved not their lives unto the death." (Revelation 12:11, KJV)*

According to Genesis 1:26, God's will and original intent was to create man in His image and after His likeness. In verse twenty-seven, man is made just as God designed. In Genesis chapter three, the serpent causes man to lose sight of his identity and authority.

The enemy wants to keep you distracted and focused on your past sins and failures. He will lie to you, making you doubt what God has said about you. He plans to kill, steal, and destroy you by any means necessary.

> *"The thief's purpose is to steal and kill and destroy; I have come that they may have life, and have it to the full." (John 10:10).*

redesigned & reintroduced

Contrary to the enemy's plans, there was a plan for a life of advantage and preeminence. This is the abundant life. It is available to all, but only those confident in their authority and identity in God can access it.

As His image bearers, you are to represent Him to the world. Your identity is not defined by your past but by your relationship with God. Through His love, you are renewed and restored. Your self-image can become distorted, making you a victim of an identity crisis or identity theft.

It is time for you to take back your identity and your authority. The enemy is not fighting you; he is at war with the God who is on the inside of you. Remember, you are in His image, so when he sees you, he sees an adversary. Exercise your authority and tell Satan not just to leave you alone but to go now.

Please do not allow him to manipulate your thinking. He thinks you are unaware of your identity and will exploit it. Let him know I know who I am and, most importantly, who I belong to. I am a child of the king, made in His image and after His likeness.

i know, i am enough

In the beginning, I wondered if I was good enough. There are still days and assignments when I wonder if God chose the right person.

redesigned & reintroduced

So many other people are much better and more gifted than I am. My only obligation is to show up, and He performs the miracles.

We do not possess the power alone to do the work, but God is at work within us. Made in His image and likeness, we are conduits of God's power and presence. If we could tap into who God has created us to be and the work we have been equipped to complete, there is no way we would continue to question God.

The assignment can be overwhelming, and insecurity will try to emerge. This is why we learn to rely on God and now ourselves. In our strength, it is too great. When we realize it is not me but God, we can go and do it with an attitude of I am enough.

When you struggle with inadequacy and imposter syndrome, return to the one who sent you, The Word. I also want to encourage and remind you that God does not call the qualified; He qualifies the called. If you feel the pressure to mimic or compare, do not. The spirit of comparison is from the enemy to keep you from doing what God has called you to complete. When we look at scripture, no two people have the same assignment. Moses was chastised for doing the same thing twice when God gave two commands. Remember, you are a designer original. Your genetic makeup is different from any other human on this planet, be it male or female. Do not become a victim or prey to the comparison trap.

redesigned & reintroduced

The religious organization I was raised in had many flaws, but they did not try to silence women and keep them from preaching the gospel. Even today, there are women who God has equipped and empowered to preach the gospel, and they are sitting silently on the sidelines because of man's errant theology. If you are a woman reading this book, God has called and chosen you for this time.

"If you keep quiet at a time like this, deliverance and relief for the Jews will arise from some other place, but you and your relatives will die. Who knows if perhaps you were made for just such a time as this?" (Esther 4:14).

Make the decision not to use your gender as an excuse or the opinions of man-made religion to keep you from pursuing your purpose. You are not less than because you are a woman. But you are a fearfully and wonderfully made threat to the enemy! If you do not, then God will find someone who is willing.

Whether you are a man or a woman, your yes could mean the difference between life and death for someone or an entire nation. God calls you to rise from despair, prepare for greatness, and declare, *"I know I am enough."*

This is your reintroduction.

FULL CIRCLE

do not make peace with
resentment or bitterness
shut the door
-Sabra

hell & heal

Hell is not just a place but also a state of mind. I was a full-time resident for many years while married and after my divorce. I thank God for my freedom. I have been set free from my past and the shame.

Healing is evidence of God at work. The benefits of being healed included freedom, joy, and peace. I was given the promise of John 10:10, an abundant life. I am speechless when I look back at where I was then and where God has me now. I take no credit for the life God has given me. When I am asked how I survived or how I defeated hell, my response is, "But God!"

I am alive today because God did not withdraw His spirit from me. There were times when he should have, but I am so grateful that he continued to give me a chance and then a second chance. Even when I wanted to give up on Him and when I gave up on myself, God never gave up on me. Like the prodigal son's father, He waited for me to return to Him.

The hell was real, but so was the healing. My testimony is even more gruesome than the details I have revealed in this book. God did not release me to share everything because this was not just a tell-all book but a manuscript that reveals God's power to heal, set free, and deliver. What God has done for me, HE can and will do for you.

hell & heal

surrender

My healing is not just about being or feeling better. It meant removing the mask and exposing myself to God, myself, and others. This full-circle journey was one of significant vulnerability. The hiding phase was over, and I was coming out with my hands up. God had so much more for me on the other side of my surrender.

More than anything, I desired freedom. I did not think I was worthy or deserving of the good things of God. Truth be told, I was unworthy and underserving of his goodness. I remained stuck because I did not know how to ask, seek, or knock on the door of heaven.

As a preacher's kid, I knew church but did not realize the significance of a personal relationship with God. Salvation is just the beginning of the story. It is a two-way exchange. We give ourselves to Him, and He gives Himself to us. He gave Himself for us, but He also wants to give His life to us.

Accepting Him means surrendering our lives, wills, and emotions to Him. Hold nothing back in the exchange. Your surrender is the only way to experience the peace that surpasses all understanding and joy unspeakable.

> *"I have told you these things so that you will be filled with joy. Yes, your joy will overflow". (John 15:11).*

hell & heal

When you surrender, you are saying not my will, Lord, but let your will be done in my life. Although I was still wearing the labels, he accepted me. He did not tell me to go and get it right and then come back. No, he welcomed me with open arms and patiently waited for me to surrender fully.

There is a misconception about what it means to surrender to God. When you surrender to man, you are losing. However, when you surrender to God, you gain more than before, and we always receive what is best: the Lord Jesus.

The posture of surrendering is both hands raised and opened. Your actions say, I give up and have nothing to give. My hands are open, and I can no longer hold onto anything. Freedom and healing look like letting go of what I have been holding onto.

lose the attachments

The Kirby vacuum cleaner is the first thing that comes to mind when I hear the word attachments. They had so many attachments for all the beautiful things they could do. The salespeople who would come to your house to do the demonstrations had to know about every attachment, how they work, and how to attach them correctly.

They would share a story about how it changed someone else's life who had bought what he was selling. Within their lengthy presentations, they would probe you, trying to learn about your needs and how they could persuade you to buy what they were selling.

They were trained to come into your homes, demonstrate the product, and close the sale. Getting the sale required the full demonstration of each attachment, even the ones you did not need then but would one day in the future. Some of the best salespeople are great at manipulating a situation so that you will do what they want, all while making it seem as though you made the best decision for you.

How often have we bought what the enemy was selling, including the attachments? Purchasing a Kirby was all-inclusive, regardless of whether you needed all the attachments. Some attachments are required to sustain a healthy lifestyle. However, some attachments are unnecessary and not good for us. The ability to discern what is good for you is imperative to your daily life in Christ.

He will order your steps, but He has also given us free will to choose for ourselves. We often choose without knowing what comes with it. When I married my husband, I had no idea what attachments would be included. Getting married requires taking the good with the bad, the pretty with the ugly, and the ups with the downs. He was a package deal, just like the Kirby vacuum cleaner.

It is easy to create attachments to the right and wrong people, but they are hard to break. Some attachments will lead to soul ties.

hell & heal

My divorce did not break the attachment. Instead, it further illuminated how attached I had become to our chaotic life. Our marriage changed me, and I knew I would never be the same. I was not only attached to the person but also to the way he made me feel.

Memory is a powerful tool or a dangerous weapon. We can live in the present but make decisions based on our past. This is the result of the pain of our present reality. Being married was comfortable, and I was already missing that feeling. How is it that what we know is best for us is the most painful to us? I was fully aware of the toxicity of my marriage, but I craved the companionship of being married.

You might say that is an addiction. That could be true. A person with an addiction will only get clean when they are tired of the way they are living. You can rip them off the streets, pay for rehab, and even sit them at the altar. Nothing will ever change until they decide to lose their attachment. It might get better for a moment or a season, but lasting change only comes when you decide enough is enough.

no regrets

If there is one thing I have determined in my life, it is to never live with regrets. Some things have happened in my past that I am not

hell & heal

proud of and would not want to repeat, but in the end, I choose not to look back with regret.

So many people regret their past relationships, decisions about a move, or job changes that they never understand the lesson God wanted them to learn through the trial. Was it a wrong choice? Maybe! But you can't go back and change it, so why torture yourself with thoughts of regret? "If I just wouldn't have...." or "If I knew then what I know now, I would...." That is a waste of time.

Every painful moment of your life has a purpose, and every wrong decision has a lesson to be learned. Learn from your mistakes and keep moving. How do you plan on growing if you never make a mistake? How will you know how to do things differently next time? Conduct an honest evaluation, own your behavior, and learn the lesson.

There is always something to learn from each trial, mistake, and challenge that life brings you. Decide today that you will say no to regrets. When you are going through difficult times, do not stop. It might not be easy, but you will reflect on these days as a time of enlightenment and spiritual growth. Stay the course.

"Be careful for nothing; but in everything by prayer and supplication with thanksgiving let your requests be made known unto God. And the peace of God, which passeth all understanding, shall keep your hearts and minds through Christ Jesus." (Philippians 4:6-7, KJV)

hell & heal

Coming full circle is when you recognize God making everything work together for your good. It would be easy for me to look back and feel guilty for staying in the marriage or the divorce. Paul encourages people like you and me.

"And we know that God causes everything to work together for the good of those who love God and are called according to his purpose for them." (Romans 8:28)

setting boundaries

Boundaries are for you, and they establish your value. How you expect to be treated is determined by the boundaries you are willing to set. It does not matter what kind of relationship you have; boundaries matter. Not setting boundaries will rob you of your power and impede your healing.

"Keep thy heart with all diligence; For out of it are the issues of life" (Proverbs 4:23, KJV)

Jesus valued and established boundaries. We should all want to be more like him. In the Bible, there were times when he would go away in private and pray. There were only a few times when he invited a few disciples to accompany him.

Setting boundaries became a priority in my recovery. The lack of boundaries hurt me more than the words and actions of any perpetrator of my trauma. The result was consistent anger and resentment towards them, mainly my husband; I hated him equally as much as I loved him. Inadvertently, I created unspoken boundaries that were loud and clear. "It is okay to say you are sorry and promise to do better but perpetuate the same behavior."

These toxic thoughts and behaviors are why we need healthy boundaries. Trust is a foundation for setting boundaries, and this can be difficult initially when you go through a traumatic experience. I encourage you to seek professional help. There is no shame in going to therapy.

Setting boundaries will allow you to heal emotionally and on a path of self-discovery. You can restore what was stolen from you during the trauma, your worth, and your identity. You get to decide what is acceptable and unacceptable.

You can have a mix of boundary types. These are not considered one size fits all. I learned to set boundaries in every area of my life. My healing process required me to set boundaries and communicate them effectively. Having boundaries does not mean someone will not break them. However, when they did, breaking the attachment was justifiable.

Sometimes, the healthiest thing for you is to disconnect. It might be painful in the beginning, but you will recover. There are two types of surgeries: elective and emergency. The elective surgery is usually planned, and you can live if you decide not to have it. Emergency surgery requires immediate action, however.

hell & heal

Procrastination could prove to be lethal. However, regardless of the type of surgery, you will be cut, and recovery is required.

forgiveness required, no exceptions

Forgiveness was discussed in a previous chapter, but I wanted to reintroduce it here as a vital healing component. The only way to truly be healed is to forgive. The effects of not forgiving are far greater than circumstances that keep you from forgiving.

    I wanted to get better and not stay bitter. I needed to get better. So that required forgiving, which many would say is unforgivable. The list was long and trauma-egregious, but I had to let it all go. My life and future depended on it.

    God began a good work in my life when I released the past. Forgiveness was my surrender. My arms were raised, hands open, letting go of the past. Open hands are also indicative of receiving. What God was about to put in my hands would be worth it all, surviving hell to live healed.

FULL CIRCLE

*if you are diligent
in the process,
God will be diligent
in the promise*
—Sabra

full circle

The journey of life is often a winding path filled with twists, turns, and unexpected detours. We all encounter challenges, growth, triumphs, and losses. It might feel like we are moving away from our goals only to return to a familiar but different place.

Coming full circle is a profound and transformative experience. It means revisiting past experiences, self-discovery, healing and redemption, and embracing renewed purpose and vision. It is about returning to where you started with greater wisdom, strength, and clarity.

Self-discovery allows you to reflect on the journey, see how far you have come, and develop an appreciation for your progress. You are learning to embrace your core identity and stripping away the superficial layers that the trials of life have peeled away. It is imperative to invite God into the process.

"Search me, O God, and know my heart; test me and know my anxious thoughts. Point out anything in me that offends you, and lead me along the path of everlasting life." (Psalm 139:23-24)

Reconciling with your past includes forgiveness, redemption, and finding peace. Revisiting the past with a heart of forgiveness is a powerful aspect of coming full circle. God has the power to redeem

full circle

the most painful parts of your story. Forgiveness and redemption will produce peace.

And finally, coming full circle will bring clarity to your purpose and vision. It is seeing the bigger picture and understanding how our experiences fit God's plan. You will gain wisdom from the journey, allowing you to renew your vision, live intentionally, and passionately embrace your calling.

"Work willingly at whatever you do, as though you were working for the Lord rather than for people. Remember that the Lord will give you an inheritance as your reward, and that the Master you are serving is Christ." (Colossians 3:23-24)

the mess created the message

Transformation begins with recognizing the mess you call life. In God's hands, your mess will not be wasted. Our chaos becomes a message of hope, resilience, and divine redemption through Him. Sharing your story will inspire and uplift others, demonstrating that no mess is beyond the reach of God's transformative power.

"I am the Lord, the God of all the peoples of the world, is anything too hard for me?" (Jeremiah 32:27)

Your healing and growth will depend on your willingness to trust God with your mess and His plans. My mess came in many forms, leaving me overwhelmed. Personal failures, broken

full circle

relationships, financial struggles, health crises, and so much more have happened. Nevertheless, nothing is too hard for God.

"Jesus looked at them intently and said, "Humanly speaking, it is impossible. But with God everything is possible." (Matthew 19:26)

I was in a difficult situation and needed help. I cried to God, "Please rescue me from this chaos!" God met me in my darkest hours when I called out to Him. But first, I had to invite Him into my mess so that I could be transformed and renewed.

"In his kindness God called you to share in his eternal glory by means of Christ Jesus. So after you have suffered a little while, he will restore, support, and strengthen you, and he will place you on a firm foundation." (1 Peter 5:10)

God thinks you are worth it all regardless of your messy past or present. When He comes to rescue you, He is not concerned with blaming the offender or shaming the victim. I also discovered that He is not coming for the mess, but He comes for the heart of the one in the mess.

In the second chapter of Mark, there is a paralyzed man lowered through the roof by his friends to be healed by Jesus. He was probably covered in debris from the ceiling; this man was obviously in a mess. However, the first thing Jesus did was forgive his sins. Jesus chose to deal with the man in the mess rather than the mess itself. He did heal him, saying, "Stand up, pick up your mat, and go

full circle

home!" Jesus could just as easily have healed and sent him on his way without addressing the sin in his life. The consequence of sin could have put him right back where he was, paralyzed and bound to his bed.

How often have you experienced God's miraculous power in your life only to return to the same bondage? This is why God transforms your mind to save your life. No matter how many times I begged God to save my marriage and heal my husband, without repentance, there were moments of reprieve from the chaos but not everlasting peace. I could not save or heal him; only God can, but by invitation only.

In John chapter 4, the woman at the well as she is identified in the story has made a complete mess of her life. Despite her past, Jesus schedules an appointment to spend time with her. She has been married five times and lives with a man who is not her husband.

Her life was quantifiably messy. She traveled outside town to draw water from the well to avoid being reminded of how messy her life was. Her usual routine of drawing water led to an unusual encounter with Jesus, a divinely orchestrated interruption. This day could have been just like all the others, but her life was about to be changed forever. He could have changed her situation, but He wanted to change her.

full circle

Before continuing her story, I want to share a familiar scripture to explain how God changes you.

"And so, dear brothers and sisters, I plead with you to give your bodies to God because of all he has done for you. Let them be a living and holy sacrifice- the kind he will find acceptable. This is truly the way to worship. Don't copy the behavior and customs of this world, but let God transform you into a new person by changing the way you think. Then you will learn to know God's will for you, which is good and pleasing and perfect." (Romans 12:1-2)

Paul gives us so much to consider in these two verses. Let's examine some of the key points. Give your bodies to God because of all he has done for you. This is a statement of reflection. You must take the time to stop and think about what God has done for you. When you recount the many ways He provided for you, rescued you, and healed you, the fitting response is to give yourself to Him.

Our bodies are to be living, holy, and pleasing. Holy means distinguished, distinct, or set apart. In Psalms 139:14, wonderfully also means distinguished and set apart. We present back to Him what He created. It is not your responsibility to become holy. Created in His image, you are already holy. You have a holy identity.

It is essential to know this so you will not be a victim of mistaken identity or the loss of your identity. A person with a mistaken identity is not living an *abundant life* or a *life pleasing to God*. You have yet to come to know and understand just who you are.

full circle

Consequently, you live like the prodigal son in a faraway country craving the buffet of the hogs you have been hired to feed. On the contrary, losing your identity could be the result of trauma, fear, or shame. At different times in my life, I was a victim of both. Thank God that I know who I am today.

Take an inventory of your life. How are you living? Are you a victim of mistaken identity, conforming to behaviors, patterning your life after the customs, identifying with the world, and living beneath your privilege? How do you identify, and with whom do you identify? Just as Paul did, I urge you to reclaim your identity.

In the King James Version, Romans 12:2 says *but be transformed by renewing your mind (emphasis added).* In Greek, the root word for renewing is completing a process. Now, let's put the pieces back together. If you have lost your identity, let God transform you into a new person by changing your thinking. Completing the process will change your words and your behaviors.

A second meaning of renewing is making something new again. For instance, I love the look and feel of a clean vehicle. When it has been cleaned inside and out, it's as if I just drove it off the lot for the first time. That is what God will do with your life: make you new again, just as you were created in Genesis 1:27 and Psalms 139:14.

Because of a one-on-one encounter with Jesus, the woman released shame and fear, and her messy life became her message. Her

full circle

testimony led her to the people and places she was trying to avoid. She was no longer a victim of her choices and had come full circle with a renewed identity.

the end to the beginning

Starting over is always challenging, or so I have been told. Nothing in my life had gone as planned, and I needed a new beginning. Life is a series of cycles with beginnings and endings. When you come full circle, the end is not just a conclusion but a gateway to a new beginning. Starting over will have its challenges, but it also indicates the end of something.

Endings are viewed with apprehension and sadness. At the end of my marriage, I was lost and struggling to cope with my new normal. The memory of my failure was playing like a reel on repeat in my mind. Not to mention the people who would not let me move forward. I realized that ending this season would mean letting go of any connectors to the past, making room for a new beginning and a spiritual rebirth. Holding on to old habits, relationships, or situations can hinder your growth.

> *"No, dear brothers and sisters, I have not achieved it, but I focus on this one thing: Forgetting the past and looking forward to what lies ahead, I press on to reach the end of the race and receive the heavenly prize for which God, through Christ Jesus is calling us."*
> *(Philippians 3:13-14)*

full circle

Endings create space for new beginnings. Pruning promotes growth. The same is true in your life. Only you can do the pruning work. You are the gardener of your heart and life.

"But forget all that- it is nothing compared to what I am going to do. For I am about to do something new. See, I have already begin! Do you not see it? I will make a pathway through the wilderness. I will create rivers in the dry wasteland" (Isaiah 43:18-19)

The work and process of starting over are only complete with spiritual rebirth. Until now, I did the work of letting go and making space. Here, I can finally rest and allow God to take complete control. Only He can reinvent, redesign, and reintroduce me.

"Therefore if any man be in Christ, he is a new creature: old things are passed away; behold, all things are become new!"
(2 Corinthians 5:17, KJV)

My rebirth came when I stopped allowing others' words and actions to keep me stuck in an expired season. Despite some people's harsh words and behaviors at church, I continued attending. God was healing me just because I kept showing up. He cleaned out the bitterness and hurt and gave me joy and peace.

Suddenly, my appetite for a deeper relationship with God returned. Mere attendance became a heartfelt desire to be in His presence. No longer willing to allow my past to define me, I was ready to lose the labels and live in my identity as a daughter of God. I

full circle

am thankful God never stopped waiting for me to recognize how much I needed Him.

The transition from the end to the beginning requires openness to change, resilience, and faith. An open heart and mind allowed me to see the potential and possibilities in my new beginning. Life changes can be unpredictable, but a resilient spirit helped me adapt and thrive. The more distant my thoughts were from the end, the stronger my faith became, and I was assured that my new beginning was God's divine plan.

"Trust in the Lord with all your heart; do not depend on your own understanding. Seek his will in all you do, and he will show you which path to take." (Proverbs 3:5-6)

Things were getting better and better with my daughter Lindsey and me. We had our routine and had adjusted to our new normal. I was busy attending church, being a mom, and working. Finally, I am starting to feel whole and content.

My life looked radically different because I was different. I was praying about my future and seeking God's will for my life. In my prayers, I asked God for the desires of my heart: to get married and be in ministry. My request seemed futile since so many people told me that having a second marriage and ministry was impossible. I had healed from people's thoughts and opinions, but this one lingered. I also considered the reality of my first attempt's failure.

full circle

I can testify that no good thing can be withheld from you when God has His hand on you. It might be held up for a season, but you will have everything God has for you. If your name is on it, you better prepare to receive it. God's redemption plan comes with a restoration clause. I will give back everything that was taken from you and then some. The last time might have been a failure, but the next time will not be like the previous time when God is in control.

Are you ready for a plot twist? When I met the man I would marry, he was an unsaved alcoholic who was not even a Christian. I told you God can do the impossible and the unbelievable. It will not always make sense to you or others.

> *"Instead, God chose things the world considers foolish in order to shame those who think they are wise. And he chose things that are powerless to shame those who are powerful."*
> *(1 Corinthians 1:27)*

I met Donnie at work, and we became friends. Unlike the people I attended church with, he always spoke positively about my life and future, was kind and considerate, and treated me well. It was an adjustment to be friends with a man like him. My father had been the only other man to treat me this way.

As a friend, I invited him to church, and he accepted. Here I was again, taking a stranger into a foreign land. When I tried to warn him about the Pentecostal style of worship, he waved it off and joked

full circle

about it. I will never forget his expression the first time someone started shouting and speaking in tongues. Nonetheless, he kept coming back with me.

On a Wednesday night, we were in service, and an older lady in the congregation approached him and asked if he would like to pray. He looked at her humbly and said, "I don't know how to pray." Taking him by the hand, she led him to the altar, and Donnie gave his heart to the Lord that night. That night would change our lives forever.

He started to learn how to pray and study the Bible. Our relationship progressed from friendship to dating. When he asked me to marry him, I gladly said yes. God had answered my prayer and silenced the naysayers. I was excited to be married again and to marry Donnie. I loved him, my family loved him, and so did Lindsey.

We married on December 26, 1992, and both served in leadership positions in my Father's church. God blessed us with two sons, Lee and Logan. For the first time in my adult life, I was a happily married woman and felt like I had a future to look forward to. The faithfulness of God is truly amazing. I was finally getting my fairytale. It wasn't the "as seen on TV" version, but the "only God could do this" version. It is the version I prefer.

full circle

who told you that you were naked?

When Donnie and I got married, it was understood that ministry was not an option for me or us. Second marriages were deemed unacceptable for preachers and pastors. This ideology almost prevented me from marrying Donnie, but I was already divorced, so there would be no ministry if I remarried or stayed single.

Life was good for us. We served quietly in the background at my father's church. Marrying Donnie was the best decision. It wasn't without some struggles, but we were committed to love, honor, and respect one another. I still needed healing, and he was patient with my process.

The more I healed, the less content I became. I could feel the familiar urgency of God's call. Why was this desire back again? I thought my calling was tied to my first husband, and when we divorced, that was the end. However, I realized that the Author of my life was holding the pen, and He was still writing my story.

After Adam disobeyed God, he heard God and went into hiding. God asked where are you? Adam responded by saying, *"I heard your voice, I was afraid, I was naked, and I hid myself" (Genesis 3:10, KJV, emphasis added).*

"Who told you that you were naked?" God asked.
I started to hear God ask me a similar question: Who told you that you were no longer called into ministry? Who told you that your

full circle

ministry was over? Like me, you may have started to believe or accept that you have become worthless. Let me ask you, "Who told you that you were worthless?"

You might be insecure about your ability and qualifications to complete the assignment. Let me ask you, "Who told you that you were incapable and unqualified?" Jeremiah faced this same challenge when God touched his mouth and put words in his mouth to speak.

"Then the Lord reached out and touched my mouth and said: Look, I have put My words in your mouth." (Jeremiah 1:9)

Like Jeremiah, my immaturity had created doubt in my heart and mind. There was no way God was going to use me. Not only did people convince me, but I also convinced myself.

"You can make many plans, but the Lord's purpose will prevail." (Proverbs 19:21).

victory is mine, the failed plans of the enemy

The job description of the enemy is to kill, steal, and destroy. He had done his job in my life, keeping me bound to my past so that he could rob me of the future. I spent years listening to the enemy's lies, dying in silence while he did all the talking. He had held my identity hostage long enough, and I broke the silence and began to declare the Word of the Lord over my life. No more would I be a prisoner to past mistakes or ashamed of the trauma, the divorce, or the pain of rejection. It was time for me to speak up and never again be silent.

full circle

God has given me everything the enemy said I could not have in abundance. I have an incredible husband, four children, and five grandsons. They are all thriving and serving in ministry. We pastor a growing church, and I minister and mentor women daily. The beginning of my story would not have predicted this outcome, *"but it is the Lord's purpose that prevails."*

The death and resurrection of Jesus give us many privileges that the enemy would like us not to exercise. For instance, we have been guaranteed freedom, redemption by the blood, restoration, and an abundant life of freedom sealed by the resurrection. Victory means freedom in all areas of life - mentally, physically, emotionally, financially, and spiritually. Satan knows that if you ever gain access to the knowledge of the Word of God that declares we win, he will have to admit defeat.

How we think is the greatest adversary to where we are destined to go. Winning the battle of the mind is on the path to a victorious life. Take every thought captive, and do not let it take you captive. The world is overloaded with negativity; do not become another contributor. As a man thinks in his heart, so is he. Ask yourself, "What do I think about me?" If you think of yourself as a failure and someone who will never do anything more than survive, then guess what—that is what you will do: be a survivor.

full circle

Pay attention to the people you surround yourself with. Evil communication corrupts good manners. I was thankful for Donnie. He had no idea how much his affirmations changed my perceptions of me and my future. My favorite scripture is from Paul's letter to the church in Corinth.

> *"At my first defense, no one stood with me, but all forsook me. May it not be charged against them. But the Lord stood with me and strengthened me... also I was delivered out of the mouth of the lion"* (2 Timothy 4:16-17, NIV).

Even when I wanted to give up on myself, God never gave up. Just as Paul wrote, *"all forsook me."* No one expected me to be the woman I am today, especially not me. There were so many times I wanted to quit and run away from the process. Instead, I stayed the course, and *"I was delivered out of the mouth of the lion."*

God has been faithful, *"He stood with me and strengthened me."* There were dark days during my marriage, following my divorce, and even after Donnie and I were married. My worst days with God are better than my best days without Him.

Those who have been redeemed must take pride in being more than conquerors. Even if it doesn't look like you've won, let me encourage and remind you that our victory happened at Calvary. The moment Jesus gave His life, we were no longer fighting for the victory but from the victory. When negative thoughts come, or the enemy

full circle

tries to persuade you otherwise, remember you have the victory and his plan failed.

the inevitable assignment

Full Circle means to return to a position or condition of the past, mainly in an inevitable form. The journey to being transparent and unmasked requires including the bad, the painful, and the good. Shame tried to rob me of my future and the opportunity to become the woman I am today.

For many years, I was suppressed and silenced by the legalistic designs of the local church. God does not renege on His word. My gifts and callings were without repentance. There was nothing anyone or I could have ever done to disqualify me from ministry. One might say it was inevitable or unable to be avoided, evaded, or escaped.

Whether at the highest peak in life or walking through the lowest valley, God has a purpose for your life. If you are not dead, then God is not done. You can only be a hostage to your past if you choose to stay there.

As a woman in ministry, I have faced many challenges. Therefore, having a healthy relationship with God was instrumental in getting to know myself and being able to hear His voice. Once I silenced the noise of shame and religious distractions, I heard Him

full circle

speak audibly and often. When shame tried to return and fear reared its head, I heard God say, "Trust me!" Two words that carry an immense weight in the life of someone like me. The more I listened, the more He spoke. His voice provided direction for my future. Then, one day, I heard Him say, "Go, preach the gospel, share your testimony, and declare freedom to the bound."

Starting my women's mentorship allowed me to fulfill the call of God. I can minister to the women God has assigned to be connected to me. I wanted to offer women who were survivors a safe place, to be honest and heal. This was not available to me when I was in my abusive marriage, starting over from a divorce, or in transition after my second marriage.

My heart was to provide support and encouragement to women at all stages of life. The mentorship is designed to provide an ally to women of all ages and walks of life. I also wanted to equip women in ministry, pushing them to break down barriers in pursuit of purpose.

God called me to preach when I was a young girl. My dad was intentional about protecting and nurturing that gift. He taught me never to settle. I want to do the same for the women whom I mentor.

As I close the book, I want to encourage both men and women with a call to public ministry. God truly needs you in the kingdom at this hour. Excuses are easy to make but hard to find. In other words,

full circle

why are you not working? People need to hear your testimony and how Jesus saved your life.

There is no need to reason away your lethargy. Just get up and go into the world and preach the gospel. Maybe you have been called to feed the poor, visit the sick, or work with children. Whatever your call is, now is the time to get to work. If you are on a leave of absence, it is time for you to get back to work.

I encourage getting a mentor if you are new or seasoned in your ministry. Ask God for guidance in finding the right person to speak life to you, hold you accountable, and not let you throw in the towel at the first sign of trouble.

I want to speak directly to the women reading this book. Women, you have been suppressed and silenced for far too long. This is your clarion: call women of God, rise and declare the word of the Lord in your communities, cities, states, and worldwide.

The fallacy perpetuated to restrict the role of women in ministry is no longer a barrier for you. Draw a line in the sand right now, and never allow anyone to silence your gift or store it in a back closet. I encourage you, women, to be brave and take a step in answering God's call.

Who was the first to testify of the resurrection? Who gave the instructions for the first miracle? Who saved an entire nation of people with one conversation with the King? The first woman

full circle

changed the world without saying a word. She ate, then passed it on to Adam, and *"he did eat"* (Genesis 3:6, KJV).

You are a woman, but you are not weak. You are strong enough, smart enough, and needed for this time. Embrace your calling, pursue your purpose, and allow the Holy Spirit to guide and empower you.

A fresh anointing is being released over women's lives who will stand for truth and boldly declare the Word of God. Dormant gifts are coming alive, and the weary are suddenly finding strength. Courage and confidence are being restored.

God is taking you back to where He first called you by name. You will begin to seek Him like you did when He first commissioned you. What was limiting you is being destroyed. Woman of God, you are being reintroduced to your ministry assignment, and this time, nothing will keep you from completing it. It is inevitable.

· FULL CIRCLE · FULL CIRCLE ·

*Do not fake it
'til you make it
act the way
you want to become
and believe you
can do all things
~Sabra*

Sabra Skidmore
MENTORSHIP PROGRAM

SABRA'S SISTERS

join now

$20/MONTH

Daily Devotions
Weekly Prayer Calls
Live Coaching
Exclusive FB Group

Made in the USA
Columbia, SC
14 February 2025